Burma:
Time for Change

Report of an Independent Task Force
Sponsored by the
Council on Foreign Relations

Mathea Falco, Chair

The Council on Foreign Relations is dedicated to increasing America's understanding of the world and contributing ideas to U.S. foreign policy. The Council accomplishes this mainly by promoting constructive debates, clarifying world issues, producing reports, and publishing *Foreign Affairs,* the leading journal on global issues. The Council is host to the widest possible range of views, but an advocate of none, though its research fellows and Independent Task Forces do take policy positions.

THE COUNCIL TAKES NO INSTITUTIONAL POSITION ON POLICY ISSUES AND HAS NO AFFILIATION WITH THE U.S. GOVERNMENT. ALL STATEMENTS OF FACT AND EXPRESSIONS OF OPINION CONTAINED IN ALL ITS PUBLICATIONS ARE THE SOLE RESPONSIBILITY OF THE AUTHOR OR AUTHORS.

The Council will sponsor an Independent Task Force when (1) an issue of current and critical importance to U.S. foreign policy arises, and (2) it seems that a group diverse in backgrounds and perspectives may, nonetheless, be able to reach a meaningful consensus on a policy through private and nonpartisan deliberations. Typically, a Task Force meets between two and five times over a brief period to ensure the relevance of its work.

Upon reaching a conclusion, a Task Force issues a report, and the Council publishes its text and posts it on the Council website, www.cfr.org. Task Force reports can take three forms: (1) a strong and meaningful policy consensus, with Task Force members endorsing the general policy thrust and judgments reached by the group, though not necessarily every finding and recommendation; (2) a report stating the various policy positions, each as sharply and fairly as possible; or (3) a "Chair's Report," where Task Force members who agree with the Chair's report may associate themselves with it, while those who disagree may submit dissenting statements. Upon reaching a conclusion, a Task Force may also ask individuals who were not members of the Task Force to associate themselves with the Task Force report to enhance its impact. All Task Force reports "benchmark" their findings against current administration policy in order to make explicit areas of agreement and disagreement. The Task Force is solely responsible for its report. The Council takes no institutional position.

For further information about the Council or this Task Force, please write the Council on Foreign Relations, 58 East 68th Street, New York, NY 10021, or call the Director of Communications at 212-434-9400. Visit our website at www.cfr.org.

CONTENTS

Foreword   v

Acknowledgments   vii

Executive Summary   1

Task Force Report   7

   Political Overview   7

   Regional Context   10

   Economic and Social Conditions   11

   Future of the Military   14

   Human Rights   15

   Key Issues and Recommendations   18

Additional and Dissenting Views   34

Task Force Members   40

Task Force Observers   45

Appendixes

   Appendix A: United Nations General Assembly
     Resolution   49

   Appendix B: European Union Common
     Position   56

FOREWORD

Burma is an important but poorly understood country. It continues to fascinate because of its unique history and culture, but decades of military misrule have left the country impoverished. For the past fifteen years, a genuine democracy movement has been alive in Burma, and the world has watched while the National League for Democracy (NLD), led by Aung San Suu Kyi, has struggled against the military junta for recognition, influence, and a share of power.

Bordering on major powers such as China and India, and with a population of 50 million, abundant natural resources, and the second largest landmass in East Asia, Burma has the potential to be a viable economy and eventually a healthy democracy. But for these things to happen, Burma must emerge from four decades of repressive rule. This Council-sponsored Independent Task Force recommends ways the United States may be able to help Burma do so.

Last year, Mathea Falco, who had first visited Burma in 1977 as assistant secretary of state for international narcotics matters, approached me about creating an Independent Task Force on Burma. I recognized that this was a particularly opportune time for us to support such an effort. In May 2002, the regime had released Aung San Suu Kyi from eighteen months of house arrest. During this period, regime officials had secret talks with her and her colleagues facilitated by a United Nations special envoy. The regime also released several hundred political prisoners. This raised hopes that the two sides would move to substantive political dialogue leading to agreement on transition to democratic government. Optimism faded, however, as talks did not resume and human rights abuses continued. In this context, the Task Force undertook its review of U.S. policy toward Burma.

The bipartisan Task Force, chaired by Mathea Falco, reflects a wide range of perspectives. Members were drawn from international business, law, media, academia, public health, and human rights advocacy groups, among other areas. We were particularly fortunate to have on the Task Force four members of Congress with a deep interest in Burma: Senator Richard Lugar (R-IN), Senator Mitch McConnell (R-KY), Senator Dianne Feinstein (D-CA), and Representative Tom Lantos (D-CA).

As you will see, the Task Force carefully considered present conditions in Burma and has come up with a series of specific recommendations for U.S. policy in four areas: humanitarian assistance to address Burma's health crisis; promoting democracy, human rights, and the rule of law; narcotics control policy; and refugees, migrants, and internally displaced persons. These recommendations are intended to inform U.S. government actions as well as to increase U.S. cooperation with other countries, especially in Asia, to bring about a long overdue political, economic, and social transformation of Burma.

My great thanks go to Mathea Falco for her time and effort as the chair and to all of the members of this Task Force for developing a report that will be a significant contribution to U.S. policymaking on Burma.

Leslie H. Gelb
President
Council on Foreign Relations
June 2003

ACKNOWLEDGMENTS

The Independent Task Force on Burma has been a collective endeavor that reflects the contributions and hard work of many individuals. Task Force members included both Council members and nonmembers drawn from diverse backgrounds, such as public health, human rights, multinational business, law, journalism, diplomacy, and academia. Some members had extensive experience in Burma, while others did not. Everyone, however, shared an active interest in U.S. policy toward Burma as well as a deep concern about that country's future.

Task Force members and observers, including many from Washington, D.C., participated energetically in three meetings that took place at the Council on Foreign Relations in New York in December 2002 and in February and March 2003. They generously shared their ideas and offered valuable suggestions on various drafts. The report reflects the views of the Task Force members, except as indicated in additional or dissenting views.

In the course of the three meetings, the Task Force heard from the ambassador of the Union of Myanmar to the United States, U Linn Myaing; the representative to the United Nations for the National Coalition Government of the Union of Burma, Dr. Thaung Htun; and the director of the Fogarty AIDS Program at Johns Hopkins University, Dr. Chris Beyrer. We appreciated their willingness to share their perspectives on the challenges currently facing Burma. The Task Force benefited greatly from their expert knowledge.

I am particularly grateful to Leslie H. Gelb, the Council's president, for his vision in establishing this Task Force on Burma. I am also indebted to his editorial suggestions, which have greatly strengthened the focus of the Task Force report. Our thanks go also to the staff of the Council, particularly to Lee Feinstein, the deputy director of studies and the director of strategic policy, who guided our efforts with unfailing good cheer, as well as to research associates Faiza Issa and Cheryl Igiri who helped early and late in the process. Research associate Sarah Saghir deserves special thanks for her tireless work in staffing the Task Force meetings as well as in managing the many drafts that preceded the final report. I would also like to thank the Arthur Ross Foundation for their generous financial support.

Mathea Falco
Chair

EXECUTIVE SUMMARY

On May 30, 2003, the Burmese military regime orchestrated violent attacks by progovernment militia on Aung San Suu Kyi, the leader of the National League for Democracy (NLD), and her supporters as they traveled outside Mandalay. At least four of her bodyguards were killed, as were a significant number of others. She has been in prison since then. Following the attacks, the regime arrested more than 100 democracy activists, imprisoned at least a dozen, shut down NLD offices across the country, and closed schools and universities. This is the bloodiest confrontation between Burma's military rulers and democracy supporters since 1988, when the government suppressed a popular uprising against the regime and thousands were killed.

Burma has been ruled for more than 40 years by a succession of military regimes that have systematically impoverished a country once known for its high literacy rate, excellent universities, and abundant natural resources. Today, Burma is one of the most tightly controlled dictatorships in the world, lacking any freedom of speech, assembly, or the press; denying any due process of law; and perpetuating human rights abuses, such as forced labor, military rape of civilians, political imprisonment, torture, trafficking in persons, and the use of child soldiers. Burma is also facing what the United Nations Children's Fund (UNICEF) has called a "silent emergency," a health crisis of epidemic proportions. HIV/AIDS is spreading rapidly, and malaria, tuberculosis, leprosy, maternal mortality, and malnutrition are pervasive. Government spending on health and education is miniscule.

Burma is a leading producer of opium and methamphetamine for the illegal drug trade, a major source of corruption within Burma. Four decades of military operations against insurgent ethnic nationalities as well as mass forced relocations have created one of the largest refugee populations in Asia. As many as two million people have fled Burma for political and economic reasons;

inside Burma, hundreds of thousands have been internally displaced. They lack access to food, health care, schools, and even clean water.

In August 1988, a popular uprising against the military regime was brutally suppressed and thousands were killed. In 1990, the regime held elections for a multiparty parliament in which the NLD, led by Aung San Suu Kyi, who was then under house arrest, won 82 percent of the seats. However, the elections were ignored by the junta and the elected parliamentary representatives never took office. The regime imprisoned hundreds of prodemocracy supporters, including elected members of parliament. Thousands more fled the country.

After the 1988 uprising, the United States imposed graduated sanctions on Burma, initially terminating economic aid, withdrawing trade preferences, imposing an arms embargo, and blocking loans and grants from international financial institutions. In 1997, based on a presidential finding that the Burmese government had committed large-scale repression and violence against the democratic opposition, the United States banned any new American investments in Burma.

In 2000, the United Nations, mandated by UN General Assembly resolutions, sent Special Envoy Tan Sri Razali Ismail to Rangoon to promote substantive political dialogue between the Burmese government and the democratic opposition on transition to a democratic government. Since then, Ambassador Razali has visited Rangoon ten times with no apparent progress toward establishing this dialogue.

In order to strengthen international efforts to install a democratic government and end repression in Burma, the Task Force recommends that the United States take specific initiatives in four key areas: humanitarian assistance to address Burma's health crisis; promoting democracy, human rights, and the rule of law; narcotics control policy; and refugees, migrants, and internally displaced persons.

Humanitarian Assistance to Address Burma's Health Crisis
In view of Burma's massive public health crisis, the United States should increase humanitarian assistance to Burma, provided that the funds are given to international nongovernmental organizations (NGOs) for basic human needs through a process that requires transparency, accountability, and consultation with the NLD and other groups representative of a multiethnic Burma.

Although the United States should not generally provide humanitarian assistance directly to the Burmese government, the United States could provide technical assistance to the Ministry of Health if the Burmese government agrees to meet the U.S. Centers for Disease Control and Prevention (CDC) standard that HIV/AIDS testing be voluntary and confidential.

The United States should work together with other donor governments, UN agencies, and, if possible, the Burmese government's State Peace and Development Council (SPDC) to establish certain minimal standards of independence for international NGOs operating in Burma, including clear guidelines for administrative operations, reporting, and other regulations involving duty-free entry privileges, memoranda of understanding, and residency permits.

Promoting Democracy, Human Rights, and the Rule of Law
In view of the recent government-sponsored attacks on members of the democratic opposition, resulting in a number of deaths, and the Burmese government's detention of Aung San Suu Kyi, the United States should urge the UN Security Council to adopt a resolution demanding the immediate release of Aung San Suu Kyi and all political prisoners and condemning the Burmese government's egregious human rights abuses as well as its refusal to engage in substantive political dialogue with the democratic opposition. In addition, the United States should urge the Security Council to hold an emergency session on Burma to discuss imposing targeted sanctions, which could include denying visas to leaders of the military regime, the Union Solidarity Development Association (USDA), and their families; freezing their assets; and imposing bans both on new investment in Burma and on the importation of goods produced in Burma.

The Burmese military government has failed to address human rights abuses—including refusing to unconditionally release all political prisoners—and has not moved forward in talks with the NLD and other prodemocracy groups toward establishing a democratic government. Because of these failures, the United States should increase well-targeted sanctions, including an import ban on goods produced in Burma, and encourage the United Nations and other countries to join with the United States in adopting similar sanctions.

The United States should redouble its efforts with the governments of China, Japan, and the Association of Southeast Asian Nations (ASEAN) countries, particularly Thailand, Singapore, and Malaysia, to press the SPDC to work with the NLD and ethnic nationalities toward political transition in Burma. The United States, as a member of the ASEAN Regional Forum, should urge ASEAN to consider seriously the cross-border effects of Burma's internal problems, such as illegal migration, health, trafficking, narcotics and other issues connected with the internal situation in Burma. The United States should also continue to coordinate its policies toward Burma with those of the European Union.

The United States should strongly discourage the government of Japan from forgiving outstanding debts from bilateral grants and loans, with the exception of those that directly address basic human needs, until the SPDC makes substantial progress in improving human rights and in engaging in substantive political dialogue with the democratic opposition. Aid for basic human needs should exclude infrastructure projects, such as dams and airport renovations. Moreover, the United States should encourage Japan to use its influence with ASEAN governments to urge them to become proactive in the support of democracy and human rights in Burma.

While maintaining its own sanctions on Burma, the United States, as one of the largest donors to the international financial institutions, should urge Asian investors to press the Burmese government to begin implementing the economic measures recommended by the World Bank, the International Monetary Fund (IMF), and the Asian Development Bank as one of the prerequisites for further investment. The United States should also urge China to use its influence to press the Burmese government to reform the country's economy and move toward democratic governance in order to promote stability in the region.

In order to develop capacity for future democratic governance and to rebuild technical competence in Burma, the United States should promote cultural, media, and educational exchanges with the Burmese, provided that these opportunities are readily accessible to all qualified candidates, including representatives of the political opposition. The selection process should include widespread publicity of exchange and fellowship opportunities, and a joint selection committee comprised of Burmese civilian authorities (academics and intellectuals) and representatives of the U.S. embassy in Rangoon who would, after consulting broadly, make their selections based on the quality of candidates and their potential to contribute to Burma's future. In addition, the United States should provide increased funding for the American Center in Rangoon as well as for English-language training and scholarship opportunities.

U.S. Narcotics Control Policy Toward Burma

The United States should not certify Burma at this time, because it has "failed demonstrably" to curtail drug production, drug trafficking, and money laundering. In addition, the United States should not provide any counternarcotics assistance to the Burmese government. Increased counternarcotics cooperation should depend, at minimum, on significant steps by the Burmese government to curb methamphetamine production, to arrest leading traffickers, and to stop channeling drug money into the licit economy.

Refugees, Migrants, and Internally Displaced Persons

The United States should strongly urge the Thai government to halt deportations of Burmese and protect the security of Burmese living in Thailand, regardless of their status. In addition, the United States should coordinate U.S. policy toward Thailand with other donors, such as the governments of Norway, Denmark, Japan, and Canada.

The United States should provide increased humanitarian assistance, including cross-border assistance, for displaced Burmese along both sides of the Thai-Burma border as well as on Burma's borders with India, Bangladesh, and China and inside Burma itself. Support should be provided for clean water, sanitation services, primary healthcare, reproductive healthcare, and health education for refugees and undocumented migrants living in refugee-like circumstances. Support for education, especially for women and children, is also critical.

The United States should urge greater access by international NGOs and UN agencies to the northern Rakhine state, on Burma's western border, to provide humanitarian assistance and monitor abuses committed against Muslim communities and repatriated refugees.

TASK FORCE REPORT

POLITICAL OVERVIEW

On May 30, 2003, the Burmese military regime orchestrated violent attacks by progovernment militia on Aung San Suu Kyi, the leader of the National League for Democracy (NLD), and her supporters as they traveled outside Mandalay. At least four of her bodyguards were killed, as were a significant number of others. She has been in prison since then. Following the attacks, the regime arrested more than 100 democracy activists, imprisoned at least a dozen, shut down NLD offices across the country, and closed schools and universities. This was the bloodiest confrontation between Burma's military rulers and democracy supporters since 1988, when the government suppressed a popular uprising against the regime and thousands were killed.

Burma has been ruled by military regimes since 1962, when General Ne Win seized power from Prime Minister U Nu. Ne Win instituted the "Burmese Way to Socialism," which systematically impoverished a country that had a 90 percent literacy rate and was rich in natural resources. Ne Win dismantled the independent judiciary, the legislature, and the multiparty system. He also effectively cut Burma off from the outside world.

Ne Win's regime spent decades engaged in military operations against the Communist Party of Burma and various ethnic minorities fighting for autonomy or independence from the central government, which has traditionally been dominated by ethnic Burmans. Even under the rule of the British Empire, however, Burma was never a unified political state, but rather an agglomeration of many ethnic groups with little in common. The British allowed the ethnic areas in upper Burma to retain their social structures, including a degree of self-governance, while ruling lower Burma with a professional civil service corps. The military government changed the country's name from Burma to Myanmar in 1989.[1]

In August 1988, a popular uprising against the military regime, which was initiated by university students in Rangoon and spread nationwide, was brutally suppressed, and thousands were killed. Aung San Suu Kyi (daughter of the national hero General Aung San, who was assassinated in 1947) emerged as an immensely popular prodemocracy leader and became the key political force in uniting much of the opposition into the NLD. The military regime, then known as the State Law and Order Restoration Council (SLORC), disturbed by growing political support for the NLD, placed Aung San Suu Kyi under house arrest in 1989. In 1990, the SLORC held elections for a multiparty parliament. The NLD won 82 percent of the seats.[2] The SLORC never allowed the new parliament to convene and instead created a National Convention, dominated by the military; the elections were ignored, and the elected parliamentary representatives never took office. The regime also imprisoned hundreds of prodemocracy supporters, including elected members of parliament. Thousands more fled the country.

In 1995, the SLORC released Aung San Suu Kyi from house arrest but severely restricted her movements as well as political activities by the NLD. The SLORC also forced many NLD members to resign and closed down NLD offices across the country. Tensions continued to build until September 2000, when the regime again placed Aung San Suu Kyi under house arrest after she tested the limits of her freedom by traveling outside Rangoon.

In May 2002, faced with disastrous economic conditions and intense pressure from the international community, the regime

---

[1] At independence in 1948, under an elected government, the country's name became the Union of Burma. In 1989, the State Law and Order Restoration Council (SLORC), which had seized power a year before, issued a decree changing the country's official name to Myanmar, an English transliteration of "Burma" from Burmese. The Burmese democracy movement, including the NLD, rejects this change. The United Nations uses the name Myanmar; however, the U.S. government continues to use the name Burma.

[2] In April 2003, President George W. Bush reiterated that the United States continues to recognize the results of the 1990 elections.

(renamed the State Peace and Development Council [SPDC] in November 1997) released Aung San Suu Kyi from house arrest. The SPDC also released several hundred political prisoners, allowed approximately 90 of the 400 NLD offices in Burma to reopen, and permitted Aung San Suu Kyi to travel around Burma for the first time in thirteen years. However, her recent trips—including ones to deliver speeches to thousands of supporters—have been marred by harassment instigated by government-affiliated political organizations and local officials.

During the eighteen-month period of Aung San Suu Kyi's latest house arrest, the SPDC leadership held secret meetings with her and her senior colleagues that were facilitated by the United Nations special envoy for Myanmar, Malaysian diplomat Razali Ismail, as mandated by United Nations General Assembly resolutions. The UN-led initiative, coupled with Aung San Suu Kyi's release in May 2002, raised hopes that the two sides would move to substantive political dialogue, together with ethnic minorities, leading to agreement on transition to democratic government. However, the regime remains unwilling to begin serious political dialogue with the NLD.

Meanwhile, General Than Shwe (the ultimate authority in the ruling junta) has consolidated his power within the military through selective dismissals and forced retirements. Observers note that Than Shwe, rarely seen in public, appears to have many similarities to Burma's reclusive, all-controlling dictator Ne Win, who died under house arrest in December 2002. Under Than Shwe's direction, the SPDC arrested a dozen democracy activists early in 2003, but then released 21 political prisoners several months later. Three of them had been incarcerated for fourteen years. (Although their sentences were completed in 1999, they continued to be held under a law that allows the government to imprison individuals without trial for security reasons.) More than 1,300 political prisoners remain behind bars.

REGIONAL CONTEXT

As the natural connection between the Indian subcontinent and East Asia, Burma occupies an important crossroad of southern Asia. It is of strategic interest to its neighbors China and India, which are rivals for influence; to Japan, which views Chinese hegemony over Burma as strengthening China to Japan's detriment; and to the Association of Southeast Asian Nations (ASEAN), which views Chinese economic penetration of Burma with some concern. The desire to reduce Chinese influence in Burma was an important consideration in ASEAN's decision to admit Burma to the organization in 1997.

China has become Burma's most important partner, offering debt relief, economic development grants, technical assistance, and soft loans used for the construction of infrastructure and light industry. China is also Burma's major supplier of arms and munitions. Chinese immigration into Burma has been extensive in the past decade: estimates of the number of Chinese now in the country range from one to two million, compared to several hundred thousand before 1988.

Thailand, which shares a 2,400-kilometer border with Burma, is the country most directly affected by Burma's social and economic problems. Illegal drug production and trafficking—particularly of methamphetamines—infectious diseases, refugees, and migrants spill over into Thailand (as well as into Burma's other neighbors in the region). Cross-border trade is extensive. Thai Prime Minister Thaksin Shinawatra, elected in July 2002, has sought closer relations with the Burmese regime. (Thaksin also has extended business interests with members of the Burmese military leadership.) Thailand, along with Singapore and Malaysia, has tried to encourage political stability and economic reforms in Burma. In May 2003, Thailand's foreign minister, Surakiart Sathirathai, publicly urged the international community to support moves by the SPDC toward reconciliation with the democratic opposition in Burma.

ECONOMIC AND SOCIAL CONDITIONS

Following World War II, Burma was poised to be the first "tiger" economy of Southeast Asia. In the late 1940s, the newly independent Burma had the best schools and universities in the region and a well-educated, highly literate population. Although devastated during the war, it was also known as the rice bowl of Asia. Today, Burma is one of the world's poorest countries.

The government does not consistently or regularly report reliable data on the economy, health, education, government spending, and other areas. Consequently, it is extremely difficult to obtain solid figures that give an accurate picture of the current situation, including the country's population. The U.S. State Department believes that Burma's population is 51 million, while other estimates are somewhat lower.

The United Nations Development Programme (UNDP) ranked Burma 118th out of 162 nations in 2001 on its Human Development Index. The World Bank reports that Burma has an average per capita GDP of approximately $300. There are multiple exchange rates. The official exchange rate set by the government is six kyat to one U.S. dollar. There is also an unofficial but generally available market exchange rate that currently stands at more than 1,000 kyat to the dollar and a foreign exchange certificate (FEC) rate below the unofficial rate. Rampant inflation (30 to 50 percent per annum) persists, reflecting long-term mishandling of the economy, continuous printing of currency in unreported amounts, extremely low foreign exchange reserves, and reliance on imports for basic necessities. Pervasive corruption, economic mismanagement, political uncertainty, and frequently changing economic policies have driven out most major foreign investors, including those from neighboring countries, such as Singapore and Malaysia, which do not have prohibitions against investments in Burma.

The most recent financial crisis began in February 2003, when the government closed a dozen private deposit companies, which precipitated a run on deposits at the larger, regular banks, such as the Asia Wealth Bank. All banks then imposed strict withdrawal limits and called on customers to repay outstanding loans. They also suspended the use of ATM machines. The government's central bank bailed out the three largest banks by printing more kyat. The banking crisis has greatly weakened already fragile individual resources and local businesses.

Primarily an agricultural economy, Burma also has substantial mineral, oil, natural gas, fishing, and timber resources. However, decades of mismanagement and corruption are rapidly depleting these assets, and the country can now barely feed its own people. A systematic policy of forced relocations of farmers and indigenous populations has also severely diminished agrarian production. These policies have impoverished the rural population and undermined food security.

Rice harvests are poor, fertilizer is lacking, and agricultural credit is underfunded. Moreover, for 30 years, the government has forced farmers to plant certain crops at specific times and to sell significant percentages of them to the state well below market prices. In April 2003, the government announced that it was scrapping this policy and removing all controls over domestic rice sales and purchases. Guidelines governing rice exports are still being developed.

The International Monetary Fund (IMF), after consultation with the staffs of the World Bank and the Asian Development Bank, has made a series of recommendations to Burma for economic reforms. They include suggestions for fiscal, monetary, and budgetary reforms; the abolition of dual exchange rates; increasing the independence of the central bank; and structural reform of state enterprises. Implementation of the IMF reform program would over time improve the economic performance of the country and the standard of living of its people. But the government has taken no action on any of the recommendations.

Although women historically played an important informal role in Burma's economy, today they are virtually invisible in major corporate enterprises, diplomacy, and politics (with the notable exception of Aung San Suu Kyi). Women are effectively absent in the higher military ranks, which precludes them from the economic benefits and privileges enjoyed by the armed forces. The handful of women in leadership positions in the military are most often wives, daughters, or other relatives of military men. Women do occupy significant positions in midlevel government administrative positions and in the teaching profession, including at university levels.[3]

The maternal mortality rate is one of the highest in Asia; more than half these deaths are from illegal abortions. One-quarter of children aged ten to fourteen work; many are forcibly conscripted into the army or government infrastructure projects. Only one-third of the country has access to clean water and sanitation.

Although the government claims to be increasing spending on education, actual spending on education has decreased dramatically (from already minimal levels) on a per capita basis, placing the burden of providing for education almost entirely on families. In 2000, the government spent less than one-half of one percent of GDP on education. According to UNICEF, 57 percent of households cannot afford basic education for their children. Only one-third of the children who do go to school complete the five years of primary school, and in many remote areas of the country, there is no education at all. No literacy surveys have been conducted for more than two decades.

The universities in Rangoon have been closed for much of the past ten years. Although the universities were officially reopened in July 2000, academic terms have been truncated and curricula accelerated to reduce the backlog of students. The government has also established a number of "universities of distance learning" in remote rural areas, often near military facilities. Students attending those institutions are essentially cut off from the social, cultural, and political activities that take place in urban centers and are under the watchful eyes of nearby military personnel.

Meanwhile, military spending has skyrocketed. The government spends far more on the military than on health and education

---

[3] The SPDC has not complied with the treaty requirements of the Convention on the Elimination of All Forms of Discrimination Against Women (CEDAW), which the government signed in 1997. CEDAW stipulates that women are not to be discriminated against in any form of state action that dilutes equality or their access to power.

combined. The World Bank, in a recent unpublished report, criticized the Burmese government for these misplaced priorities and called for reforms in both governance and economic policies. Burma, once considered one of Asia's most literate societies, has deteriorated into a state of marginal literacy, with dysfunctional educational programs.

FUTURE OF THE MILITARY

Resolving the role of the military is a central issue in determining Burma's future. The armed forces in Burma, known as the Tatmadaw, have more than doubled in size since the 1988 uprising, when the government undertook a major military expansion and modernization campaign. The military—now amply equipped with weapons and aircraft bought primarily from China—is able to carry out extended operations against insurgencies in the countryside, civil disturbances in the cities, and external threats on its borders. In recent years, the regime has negotiated cease-fires with most of the main insurgent groups they have been fighting for decades. The SPDC's announcement last year that it was purchasing ten Russian-made MIG aircraft and a nuclear reactor, reportedly for research purposes, led to international expressions of concern regarding the junta's policy of continuing arms acquisitions despite the country's severe economic problems.

The Tatmadaw (estimated to have about 400,000 members) consumes more than 40 percent of the government's annual budget, according to the World Bank. Its members occupy the top positions in almost every government agency. The military has extensive economic interests, including in the tourist trade, specifically in many large hotels, and in manufacturing enterprises that produce goods for both civilian and military needs. Only military personnel are eligible to own shares in the military-operated corporations that are significant forces in the economic and financial life of the country. These conglomerates are the Myanmar Economic Holdings Corporation and the Myanmar Economic Corporation, created by special edict and completely under military authority.

Through these organizations, which employ hundreds of thousands of workers, the military has extensive joint ventures with foreign firms.

It is doubtful that the regime would voluntarily cede power to democratically elected politicians without guarantees of maintaining significant power over critical issues, including its own operations, its economic interests, and the unity of the state. It will likely also require guarantees against retribution from any civilian government. The Burmese military contends that the armed forces are necessary to hold the country together, to maintain internal stability, and to protect the country from external threats as well as from terrorism. Despite Aung San Suu Kyi's reassurances that the NLD would not pursue recriminations against them, some top military men may fear the loss of their extensive privileges and economic advantages as well as reprisals by any future government not controlled by the military.

HUMAN RIGHTS

The military regime is regularly condemned by the United States, other governments, the United Nations, and international human rights organizations for its egregious human rights abuses. Burma remains one of the most tightly controlled dictatorships in the world, lacking any freedom of speech, assembly, or the press; denying any due process of law; and continuing to practice such abuses as arbitrary political imprisonment, torture, mass forced relocations, and forced labor. Since April 2001, the United Nations special rapporteur on the human rights situation in Myanmar, Professor Paulo Sergio Pinheiro, has met periodically with government officials, Aung San Suu Kyi, and other NLD and ethnic minority leaders to address human rights abuses. Pinheiro has also explicitly called for a process of political liberalization that has yet to be addressed by the regime.

Although the SPDC has released several hundred political prisoners since Ambassador Razali's initiative to promote reconciliation talks between the SPDC and the NLD began in 2000, more than 1,300 remain incarcerated. Professor Pinheiro has expressed disappointment with the lack of progress. He cut short his most recent visit in March 2003 after finding a microphone in a room he was using to interview political prisoners. General Khin Nyunt, one of the junta's top three generals, subsequently apologized for the incident. It is not clear when Pinheiro will return to Burma.

Political Prisoners

The Burmese government continues to arrest and incarcerate democracy supporters, including students and old people. Those arrested do not benefit from due process and are often given long sentences without trial or legal representation. Those released from prison are made to sign a pledge that they will not engage in activity "detrimental to the public order."

Prison conditions are deplorable and life threatening. In 1999, for the first time, the government allowed the International Committee of the Red Cross to visit all 35 prisons in Burma and about half of the estimated 100 labor camps. In January 2003, Amnesty International representatives were allowed inside Burma for the first time. (During their visit, the police arrested twelve more political activists, including seven NLD members, for "antigovernment" activities.)

Forced Labor

For the past decade, the International Labour Organization (ILO) has steadily increased pressure on the Burmese government to honor its international treaty commitments to prohibit the use of forced labor. In 1998, the ILO found that the Burmese regime practiced "widespread and systematic" use of forced labor, which particularly targeted ethnic nationalities living in border regions. In 1999, the ILO adopted a resolution barring Burma from ILO meetings and technical assistance, noting that the SPDC continued "to inflict the practice of forced labor, nothing but a contemporary form of slavery, on the people of Myanmar." In November 2000, the ILO concluded that the government of Burma had not taken effective action to end the practice of forced labor and, for the first time in its history, called on all ILO members (governments, workers, and business entities) to take measures to ensure that their relations with the regime do not contribute to the use of forced labor in Burma. In September 2002, the ILO posted a liaison officer in Rangoon to work with the Burmese government to develop a plan to eliminate forced labor. However, in March 2003, the liaison officer reported to the ILO that no progress had been made in developing an adequate plan and that forced labor persists. The ILO has repeatedly condemned the Burmese regime for its intolerance of freedom of association. The ILO has concluded that independent trade unions are not allowed in Burma and that any worker attempting to exercise this basic human right is persecuted by the regime.

Military Rape of Civilians
Violence by soldiers against villagers has been widespread during decades of military suppression in the dissident ethnic (non-Burman) areas beyond Rangoon. However, sexual violence in particular has escalated dramatically in recent years. The U.S. Department of State and human rights organizations contend that the military uses rape systematically as a weapon of war, which, if confirmed, would constitute the kinds of war crimes that the International Criminal Court was set up to prosecute. Reports by the U.S. Department of State, Human Rights Watch, Amnesty International, and Refugees International confirm the widespread, systematic use of rape by the military, particularly in remote areas where regional military commanders have considerable autonomy. Shan nongovernmental organizations (NGOs) have found that during the past several years, more than 600 women and girls have been raped by Burmese soldiers in the Shan state (the largest of the seven ethnic nationality states). Most of these rapes were committed on military bases by officers. One-quarter of the rape victims were subsequently murdered. Refugees International and Christian Solidarity Worldwide have also reported military rapes of Mon, Karen, and Karenni women and girls. The government denies that these rapes have occurred. UN Special Rapporteur Pinheiro is seeking to conduct an independent investigation.

Trafficking in Persons and Child Soldiers

Burma is a major source for international trafficking in the sex trade and in domestic and factory work, principally in Thailand, China, Taiwan, Malaysia, Pakistan, and Japan. The 2002 U.S. State Department report on trafficking in persons classified Burma as a Tier 3 country, which is defined as one that is not making significant efforts to comply with the minimum standards set out in the U.S. Trafficking Victims Protection Act of 2000. Burma has no comprehensive antitrafficking law, and the laws relating to kidnapping and prostitution are never used against regime officials.

Burma is the world's largest single user of child soldiers, most of whom are forcibly recruited from rural villages. Although some insurgent groups also use child soldiers, the Burmese army is the principal offender. Rangoon came under criticism recently after UNICEF released a report estimating that as many as 70,000 child soldiers are in the national army. Human Rights Watch issued a detailed report on child soldiers in October 2002 affirming that some of the child soldiers, who constitute one-fifth of Burma's army, are as young as eleven years old. The report also noted much less extensive use of child soldiers by ethnic minority armies relative to their use by the Burmese army. Although Burma ratified the UN Convention on the Rights of the Child in 1991, the military continues to ignore its provisions, including those prohibiting the use of child soldiers.

KEY ISSUES AND RECOMMENDATIONS

Humanitarian Assistance to Address Burma's Health Crisis

Burma is experiencing what UNICEF has called a "silent emergency," facing a rampant HIV/AIDS epidemic and declining life expectancy. Malaria, tuberculosis, leprosy, and malnutrition are pervasive, as are maternal mortality and morbidity, unsafe abortion, and sexually transmitted diseases. Drug abuse, including intravenous drug use, is a growing problem. Although the government maintains that there are only about 90,000 addicts in Burma, UN surveys indicate that the addict population could be as large as 500,000.

Burma has the highest adult HIV rate in Asia, with the exception of Cambodia, where HIV infection rates are now on the decline. UN Special Rapporteur Pinheiro reported last year to the UN that the speed at which HIV/AIDS has spread in Burma is truly alarming, with almost one in every 100 persons in danger. According to the Joint UN Program on HIV/AIDS (UNAIDS), about half a million people in Burma are living with HIV. The epidemic, which is widespread and increasing, is driven by many factors, including the multiple use of needles (even in hospitals); intravenous heroin use with shared, dirty needles; sex trafficking; and rape.

Certain government policies have exacerbated Burma's health crisis. The forced displacement of hundreds of thousands of people has made them more vulnerable to infectious diseases. Forced displacement is also a major factor in pushing Burmese women into the sex trade, which helps fuel the AIDS epidemic—as does sexual violence by Burmese soldiers, such as the rapes of ethnic minority women like those reported in the Shan state.

Government spending on health is miniscule: the World Health Organization (WHO) has ranked Burma's health care system as the world's second worst, better only than Sierra Leone's. The WHO suggests that least-developed countries put 5 to 8 percent of GDP into health care at a minimum. In Burma, health expenditures fell from less than 0.38 percent of GDP in 1994 to 0.17 percent in 2000. As a result, most citizens must pay for what little treatment they can get. Because of laws that forbid the Burmese from forming independent organizations, private citizens and communities cannot organize self-help efforts to compensate for the government's inaction.

There is a clear consensus that the people of Burma need help from the outside world to meet basic humanitarian needs. Last year, the U.S. Congress appropriated $1 million to be channeled entirely to international NGOs such as Population Services International, for HIV/AIDS programs in Burma. Congress is continuing its support this year, with the provision that no humanitarian assistance pass through the government. United Nations agencies, including UNICEF and the UNDP, and a handful of international NGOs are operating in the country for this purpose. The

Global Fund to Fight Aids, Tuberculosis, and Malaria recently grant-ed $7 million to the government for tuberculosis programs.

In April, UNAIDS announced a three-year, $51 million HIV/AIDS program in Burma, involving UN agencies, Burmese government departments, and international and national NGOs. The United Kingdom has committed $15.7 million to this UNAIDS program. According to the U.K. Foreign and Commonwealth Office, current U.K. policy is to deliver "targeted, transparent, and account-able assistance to ordinary Burmese people through the UN, international NGOs, and not through the Burmese authorities," because the British state that they are not satisfied that funding delivered through the Burmese authorities would be effectively used or accounted for. The British have announced that their recent con-tribution was made after full consultation with the NLD and that their continuing coordination meetings in Rangoon include rep-resentatives of Burmese political parties, including the NLD and members of the Chin, Arakanese, and Mon parties. Other gov-ernments have also supported public health efforts and have also generally avoided channeling aid directly through the Burmese gov-ernment, primarily to prevent diversion of funds by the military.

When donors have offered to provide aid to Burmese govern-ment agencies, the SPDC has refused to meet their basic require-ments. In 2002, the Centers for Disease Control and Prevention (CDC) offered to help Burma's Ministry of Health set up an AIDS surveillance system. But the SPDC has not agreed to the CDC standard that AIDS testing be voluntary, the results confidential, and that testing be coupled with counseling and education.

The SPDC has sought to channel foreign assistance through government agencies. However, in lieu of working directly with SPDC agencies, some international humanitarian assistance efforts are associated with government-organized nongovern-mental organizations (GONGOs), such as the Myanmar Mater-nal and Child Welfare Association (directed by the wife of SPDC General Khin Nyunt), and other large organizations, particular-ly the Union Solidarity Development Association (USDA). These groups are seen as an extension of the regime, providing social and economic benefits to those who demonstrate political loyalty more often than to those who are needy.

In 2002, UN Special Rapporteur Pinheiro proposed establishing a functional committee under UN auspices to monitor and evaluate assistance provided to Burma. This committee, according to Pinheiro, could be "one element of the trust-building process initiated through the dialogue between the Government and the NLD, thereby linking national peace and reconciliation promotion and political consultation and participation of key stakeholders: the government, the democratic opposition, ethnic groups, NGOs, and women. At the same time, such a committee could create a favorable environment for international assistance to the country." To date, SPDC Chairman General Than Shwe has not responded to this proposal.

The burden of responding to Burma's humanitarian crisis is likely to fall in the near term to UN agencies and international NGOs. These agencies face challenges maintaining their independence inside Burma. Each must negotiate the terms of its work with the SPDC. The government watches foreign staff and strictly controls travel into the country and within it. The constant threat of expulsion from the country if an agency displeases SPDC officials also tends to constrain the agencies' ability to effectively deliver assistance.

Humanitarian assistance alone is not sufficient to safeguard the health of Burma's citizens. Absent any interest on the part of the SPDC in providing health care and education, such efforts are short-term responses to longer-term problems. The current budgetary priorities of the SPDC are clear: the junta spends hundreds of millions of dollars on arms rather than on education or health care for its own people. The government also has not developed an infrastructure within the country that would allow effective delivery of humanitarian assistance. Under current circumstances, it is very difficult for outside donors to assist in building this infrastructure without having funds diverted by the military to its own purposes.

These circumstances argue for maintaining a cautious approach to providing humanitarian assistance, making sure that funds— including those supporting UN programs—are monitored so that they reach those most in need. In Burma, involving the NLD and other groups representative of a multiethnic Burma is important from a public health perspective, because many Burmese do not trust the government, particularly on sensitive issues like AIDS. This process would generate public confidence in health projects and encourage international NGOs and UN agencies to address key concerns, such as health education, reproductive health services, and programs for girls and women subjected to violence and sexual abuse, among others.

Recommendations
In view of Burma's massive public health crisis, the United States should increase humanitarian assistance to Burma, provided that the funds are given to international NGOs for basic human needs through a process that requires transparency, accountability, and consultation with the NLD and other groups representative of a multiethnic Burma.

Although the United States should not generally provide humanitarian assistance to the SPDC, the United States could provide technical assistance to the Ministry of Health if the Burmese government agrees to meet the CDC standard that HIV/AIDS testing be voluntary and confidential.

The United States should work together with other donor governments, UN agencies, and, if possible, the SPDC to establish certain minimal standards of independence for international NGOs operating in Burma, including clear guidelines for administrative operations, reporting, and other regulations involving duty-free entry privileges, memoranda of understanding, and residency permits.

Promoting Democracy, Human Rights, and the Rule of Law
Despite continuing pressure from the United Nations, the European Union (EU), Canada, the United States, and many other nations, the Burmese government has not addressed its egregious, systematic violations of human rights. Abuses include forced labor, rape, arrests, torture, intimidation, forced relocations of ethnic nationalities from their indigenous lands, and incarceration of political prisoners.

Moreover, the Burmese government appears unwilling to begin substantive talks with the NLD regarding transition to democracy. The positive international response to the SPDC's release of several hundred political prisoners and Aung San Suu Kyi from house arrest last year now seems to have been overly optimistic, particularly in light of the government-sponsored attacks on Aung San Suu Kyi and her supporters on May 30, resulting in a number of deaths and the regime's detention of Aung San Suu Kyi.

In view of the clear lack of political will on the part of the Burmese government to agree to a timetable for the return of democracy, the EU decided in April 2003 to expand its existing sanctions by increasing the number of Burmese citizens on a visa blacklist and strengthening its arms embargo against the country. The EU had already banned all contacts with members of the junta and imposed economic sanctions, including EU opposition to loans to Burma by international financial institutions and a ban on EU trade benefits.

Quite apart from government sanctions, major United States corporations are also imposing boycotts on Burma. More than 40 American companies have pulled out of Burma. Recently, department store chains Saks Fifth Avenue and the May Company have banned the sale of Burmese products in their stores. The American Apparel and Footwear Association, which includes more than 800 apparel and textile companies, announced in April 2003 that due to the repressive nature of the regime in Burma, it was calling for an immediate and total ban on U.S. textiles, apparel, and footwear imports from Burma. The association also cited the ILO finding that the Burmese regime uses forced labor—including child labor—restricts worker rights, and bans unions.

The United States has imposed graduated sanctions on Burma since the military suppressed the prodemocracy uprising in August 1988. Shortly afterward, the United States terminated direct economic aid, withdrew trade preferences, imposed an arms embargo, and blocked loans and grants from international financial institutions, such as the World Bank, the IMF, and the Asian Development Bank. After the U.S. Senate refused to confirm the nomination of two ambassadors following the departure of U.S.

Ambassador Burt Levin in 1990, the level of U.S. representation in Rangoon was downgraded from ambassador to chargé d'affaires. In 1996, the United States prohibited visas for senior members of the Burmese military and their families, and in 1997, the United States banned any new investments in Burma. The ban on new U.S. investments was triggered by a presidential finding that the Burmese government had committed large-scale repression and violence against the democratic opposition. Many analysts believe that the regime's desire to see sanctions against them eased was a key factor in its decision to release Aung San Suu Kyi from house arrest last year and to engage with UN Special Envoy Razali. Nevertheless, the regime has not changed its fundamental policies and continues to resist change.

Although there is no universal agreement regarding the effectiveness of well-targeted sanctions, there are clear examples where sanctions have bolstered the efforts of democratic movements seeking political change, including in Poland and South Africa. Sanctions put economic pressure on repressive governments, give hope to the democratic opposition inside the country, and focus international attention on human rights abuses and suppression of democracy. Sanctions also demonstrate within the country—where radio broadcasts from outside its borders are a primary source of popular information—that the international community actively supports the prodemocracy groups.

From a practical perspective, economic sanctions against the Burmese regime adversely affect industries that directly benefit the military and deprive it of an important source of revenue. An import ban would clearly have such an impact. More than a quarter of Burma's total exports go to the United States (estimated to be about $471 million). The largest portion of this trade is in textiles, produced in factories owned in whole or in part by military-affiliated companies.

The population also pays a price when sanctions are imposed. Thousands of Burmese are employed in the garment and textile industries; new sanctions would likely eliminate many jobs. At the same time, workers in Burmese garment factories, who reportedly earn considerably less than a dollar a day, reap only the smallest fraction of the benefits of exports in this sector. The Burmese economy as a whole is not organized in a manner that would make Burmese citizens significant beneficiaries of any increases in foreign investment and trade.

Pervasive corruption and continuing economic mismanagement by the regime have hurt the Burmese people even more than sanctions. They also have arguably had a greater impact on foreign investment and trade. In the past year, major foreign investors that had a large stake in the Burmese economy, including those from Singapore and Malaysia, have pulled out because of deteriorating business and political conditions.

Perhaps the most important practical argument for sanctions is that they support the Burmese democratic opposition's efforts to seek change. The ability of the democratic opposition to gain concessions from the regime is strengthened by its ability to generate international pressure on the SPDC. So long as sanctions remain in place, the military government will know it cannot achieve its economic goals without first striking a deal with the opposition.

The NLD is the legitimate representative of the people of Burma, having successfully competed against the military junta and other parties in parliamentary elections in May 1990. U.S. policy has sought to empower the NLD and its leader, Aung San Suu Kyi, both in Burma and around the world.[4] Sanctions are an essential part of U.S. policy. So, too, are U.S. efforts to increase pressure on the regime both from the United Nations and from China, Japan, Burma's ASEAN neighbors, and some European countries that still have significant economic interests in Burma. At the same time, expanding cultural and intellectual exchanges as well as educational opportunities for those inside Burma is critically important to help strengthen the nation's capacity for future democratic governance. Most Burmese under the age of 50 have

---

[4] In a statement congratulating Freedom Forum award winner Aung San Suu Kyi in April 2003, President George W. Bush affirmed that "the U.S. continues to recognize the results of the 1990 elections and supports her goals to restore democracy and national reconciliation through effective political dialogue with the ruling military regime."

had no exposure to democracy and no experience or knowledge of voting, open debate, dissent, and other aspects of civil society. In addition, the virtual collapse of the Burmese educational system, which was once the pride of Asia, has left several generations largely unequipped to guide Burma into the modern world.

Recommendations
In view of the recent government-sponsored attacks on members of the democratic opposition, resulting in a number of deaths, and the Burmese government's detention of Aung San Suu Kyi, the United States should urge the United Nations Security Council to adopt a resolution that demands the immediate release of Aung San Suu Kyi and all political prisoners and condemns the Burmese government's egregious human rights abuses as well as its refusal to engage in substantive political dialogue with the democratic opposition. In addition, the United States should urge the Security Council to hold an emergency session on Burma to discuss imposing targeted sanctions, which could include denying visas to leaders of the military regime, the USDA, and their families; freezing their assets; and imposing bans both on new investment in Burma and on the importation of goods produced in Burma.

In view of the failure of the Burmese military government to address human rights abuses—including its refusal to release unconditionally all political prisoners—and its failure to move forward in talks with the NLD and other democratic groups toward establishing a democratic government, the United States should increase well-targeted sanctions, including an import ban on goods produced in Burma, and encourage the United Nations and other countries to join with the United States in adopting similar sanctions.

The United States should redouble its efforts with the governments of China, Japan, and the ASEAN countries—particularly Thailand, Singapore, and Malaysia—to press the SPDC to work with the NLD and ethnic nationalities toward political transition in Burma. The United States, as a member of the ASEAN Regional Forum, should urge ASEAN to consider the cross-border effects of

Burma's internal problems, such as illegal migration, health, trafficking, narcotics, and other issues connected with the internal situation in Burma. The United States should also continue to coordinate closely with the EU on policies toward Burma.

Until the SPDC makes substantial progress in improving human rights and engaging in substantive political dialogue with the democratic opposition, the United States should strongly discourage the government of Japan from forgiving outstanding debts from bilateral grants and loans, except of those that directly address basic human needs. Such aid for basic human needs should exclude infrastructure projects, such as dams and airport renovations. The United States should also encourage Japan to use its influence with ASEAN governments to urge them to become proactive in the support of democracy and human rights in Burma.

While maintaining its own sanctions on Burma, the United States, as one of the largest donors to the international financial institutions, should urge Asian investors to press the SPDC to begin implementing the economic measures recommended by the World Bank, IMF, and the Asian Development Bank as one of the prerequisites for further investment. The United States should also urge China to use its influence to press the Burmese government to reform the country's economy and move toward democratic governance in order to promote stability in the region. The SPDC should not be rewarded by its Asian neighbors for economic mismanagement and poor governance.

In order to develop capacity for future democratic governance and to rebuild technical competence in Burma, the United States should promote cultural, media, and educational exchanges with Burmese, such as the Eisenhower Fellowships and the Fulbright Exchange Program, provided that these opportunities are readily accessible to qualified candidates, including representatives of the political opposition. The selection process might include widespread publicity of exchange and fellowship opportunities and a joint selection committee comprised of Burmese civilian authorities (academics and intellectuals) and representatives of the U.S. embassy in Rangoon who, after consulting broadly, base their choices on the quality of candidates and their potential to contribute to Burma's future. In addition, the United States should provide increased funding for the American Center in Rangoon as well as for English-language training and scholarship opportunities.

U.S. Narcotics Control Policy Toward Burma

Burma is the world's second largest producer of illicit opium, surpassed only by Afghanistan. According to the U.S. State Department's 2003 International Narcotics Control Status Report, a sustained drought in opium-producing areas and limited eradication efforts have combined to depress opium production levels over the past several years. In 2002, estimated opium production in Burma totaled approximately 630 metric tons, less than a quarter of the 2,560 metric tons produced in 1996.

Although opium production in Burma has declined significantly in recent years, illegal methamphetamine production has increased dramatically. In 2002, Burma exported an estimated 700 million methamphetamine tablets, primarily to Thailand and China. Methamphetamine abuse, widespread in the region, is now epidemic in Thailand, affecting more than three million Thai. The production and trafficking of narcotics from Burma has helped fuel an HIV/AIDS pandemic in the region. The drug trafficking from Burma also led to border skirmishes last year between the Burmese and the Thai armed forces after the Thai government closed key border points for several months. Thai Prime Minister Thaksin, elected in July 2002, has developed close relations with the SPDC generals, with whom he has extensive private business connections. In early 2003, the Thai government instigated a nationwide crackdown on drug dealers, resulting in more than 2,200 deaths. (The Thai government has stated that its security forces were not responsible for the killings.) Both the United Nations special rapporteur on extrajudicial executions and several international human rights groups have called attention to the Thai government's failure to follow even minimal due process standards in its drug-enforcement campaign.

The Asian Development Bank's 2002 report, which criticized the Burmese government for its failed economic policies, noted, "The economy has been propped up to a large degree from the illegal trade in opium and methamphetamine, which some observers say constitutes 20 percent of all business in the country." Drugs have been a major source of income for the United Wa State Army (UWSA), which operates along the Thai-Burma border. In the poorest areas of the country, opium poppy farming is often the only means of livelihood.

The drug trade is a major source of corruption within Burma. According to the U.S. State Department's 2003 International Narcotics Control Status Report, ". . . the prominent role of the family of notorious narcotics traffickers (e.g., Lo Hsing Han Clan), and the continuance of large-scale narcotics trafficking over years of intrusive military rule have given rise to speculation that some senior military leaders protect or are otherwise involved with narcotics traffickers." Despite persistent reports that officials in drug-producing areas are involved in or profit from drug trafficking, no Burmese military officer over the rank of full colonel has ever been prosecuted for drug offenses. Major drug kingpins invest openly in the legal economy. Money laundering is believed to be an important source of funds for business development, including joint ventures between the government and businesses such as the Asia World Company.

The United States has not provided direct narcotics control assistance to Burma since 1988. Very limited funding is provided to the United Nations Drug Control Program (UNDCP) for crop substitution efforts in border areas of Burma. Nor has the United States "certified" Burma for cooperating with the United States in curtailing illicit production and trafficking since the certification legislation was adopted in 1986.

Certification decisions are made annually. In effect, Burma's failure to be certified means that the country is ineligible for U.S. arms sales, provision of agricultural commodities (other than food), financing from the Export-Import Bank, and most types of U.S. foreign assistance. The two exceptions are narcotics control aid and humanitarian assistance. In addition, the United States must veto proposed loans to Burma by the international financial institutions, such as the World Bank and the Asian Development Bank, which effectively blocks all assistance. In January 2003, the administration announced that it would not certify Burma this year because the government's counternarcotics performance in 2002 "remained inadequate" despite progress in some areas, such as the adoption in June 2002 of a new money-laundering law. Specifically, large-scale drug production and trafficking have continued, and the government has failed to take significant steps to curtail trafficking by the UWSA, the largest trafficking organization in the country.

Recommendations
The United States should not certify Burma at this time, because it has "failed demonstrably" to curtail drug production, drug trafficking, and money laundering. In addition, the United States should not provide any counternarcotics assistance to the Burmese government. Increased counternarcotics cooperation should depend, at a minimum, on significant steps by the Burmese government to curb methamphetamine production, to arrest leading traffickers, and to stop channeling drug money into the licit economy.

Refugees, Migrants, and Internally Displaced Persons
For four decades, the military government has fought to suppress various insurgent ethnic nationalities in the border regions. In 1996, the SPDC escalated military operations in an effort to eliminate all remaining armed opposition by ethnic groups. The flow of refugees into Thailand and, to a lesser extent, India and Bangladesh (from Burma's western border) greatly increased and continues now, even after the regime has managed to subdue most of the insurgent areas. Despite the regime's having signed cease-fire agreements with many ethnic leaders, human rights abuses continue unabated, fueling the exodus of refugees and displaced persons. Since 1988, when more than 10,000 students and other activists fled Burma following the military's suppression of the prodemocracy uprising, Thailand has been the primary base of activity for exiled Burmese democracy organizations. Although some of these leaders now have legitimate travel documents issued by third countries, the vast majority are essentially stateless, leaving them vulnerable to periodic crackdowns by the Thai government. In July 2002, the Thai government

adopted a security directive to impose a ban on Burmese prodemocracy and human rights groups operating in Thailand. This included restricting visas for Burmese passport holders and the arrest and deportation of Burmese prodemocracy activists. Thai policy now threatens the security of most Burmese living in Thailand.

Thailand is not a signatory to the 1951 Convention Relating to the Status of Refugees, and its 1967 protocol leaves all refugees outside the camps in legal and literal limbo. This has created a colossal problem of identifying and registering the enormous displaced population. Although Thailand is reluctant to take any steps that might attract more refugees into the country, the large number of those present attest to the fact that lack of protection is not a deterrent and may only serve to harm the long-term health, education, and well-being not only of the refugees and migrants but also of the citizens of Thailand.

The Thai government and the international community classify people from Burma into categories that determine their legal status as well as the kind of support they might receive. The narrowest category is "refugee," defined by the Thai government as a person who was fleeing fighting when he or she left Burma. The total refugee-camp population in Thailand now totals around 143,000 (most of them Karens and Karennis). Financial support for the refugees comes from a broad base of donors, including governments and international NGOs, like the International Rescue Committee. In addition, relief workers estimate that as many as two million people (not classified as refugees) have fled Burma for political and economic reasons. These "migrants," most of whom arrived illegally, include Mons, Shans, and other minorities whose villages have been systematically destroyed by the Burmese army.

Inside Burma, hundreds of thousands of people have been internally displaced. As much as a third of the populations of the Karen, Kayah, and Shan states have fled their homes during prolonged fighting or were forcibly removed by the military for resettlement in other areas. This displaced population trapped inside Burma along the border with Thailand is subjected to forced labor, extortion, destruction of crops, torture, and killings. Unreachable by international NGOs working inside Burma, they can obtain medical services only by cross-border assistance from Thailand, which currently is minimal. The Burmese Border Consortium (BBC) estimates that there are more than 600,000 internally displaced persons along the western Thai border. Most experts believe this is a conservative figure.

More than 250,000 Muslim Rohingya refugees from Burma's Rakhine state fled persecution into Bangladesh from 1991 to 1993. Though most have since returned and the UN High Commissioner for Refugees (UNHCR) is allowed to conduct some monitoring, they continue to suffer forced labor and restrictions on their movement and religious activities. They are denied citizenship rights in Burma and are de facto stateless persons.

There is an acute need for services among the internally displaced ethnic minorities in Burma as well as among the Burmese refugees and migrants inside Thailand. The Thai government's strict classification of "refugees" as persons fleeing from recent fighting, which governs refugees' access to the Thai government–sanctioned border camps, and the government's lack of protection for refugees inside Thailand further endangers a population that has fled political persecution, human rights abuses, and forced labor. Except for people living in the camps, the majority of refugees and migrants lack access to the most minimal health care, schools for their children, and in many instances even clean water; they can survive only as an indentured, severely exploited labor force. Whole sectors of the Thai economy, including offshore fishing, seafood processing, plantation/agricultural work, and domestic services, largely depend on illegal Burmese migrant workers. Human rights and labor abuses abound: forced overtime, illegal deductions of pay, subminimum wages, physical beatings, sexual harassment and rape, forced servitude, and murder.

Women and girls are in a particularly precarious situation. The relative ease with which young women find work in Thailand, when compared to the disastrous political and economic conditions in Burma, has forced tens of thousands of young women to seek work in Thailand as commercial sex workers, factory workers, and domestic servants. Many are adolescent girls whose families cannot support them. Legal status problems complicate an already dangerous situation for trafficked children; if they are forced back into Burma or return voluntarily, there is no system there to assist them.

Recommendations
The United States should strongly urge the Thai government to halt deportations of Burmese and protect the security of Burmese living in Thailand, regardless of their status.

The United States should provide increased humanitarian assistance, including cross-border assistance, for displaced Burmese along both sides of the Thai-Burma border as well as on Burma's borders with India, Bangladesh, and China and inside Burma itself. Support should be provided for clean water, sanitation services, primary health care, reproductive healthcare, and health education for refugees and undocumented migrants living in refugee-like circumstances. Support for education, especially for women and children, is also critical.

The United States should maintain close contact with the Thai government concerning its policies toward Burmese exiles living in Thailand. In addition, the United States should coordinate U.S. policy toward Thailand with other donors, such as the governments of Norway, Denmark, Japan, and Canada.

The United States should urge greater access by international NGOs and UN agencies to northern Rakhine state to provide humanitarian assistance and monitor abuses committed against Muslim communities and returned refugees.

ADDITIONAL AND DISSENTING VIEWS

As elected officials serving in the U.S. Congress on committees with oversight of foreign affairs, we offer the following additional views on Burma:

Burma's myriad problems are rooted in political crises directly caused by the illegitimate and repressive rule of the State Peace and Development Council (SPDC). This includes a failed economy, narcotics production and trafficking, the exploitation of women and children through forced labor and conscription, gross human rights abuses, and an exploding HIV/AIDS infection rate. Those who advocate resolution of Burma's problems outside this political context serve only to prolong the suffering of the people of Burma.

The best and only hope for reconciliation and meaningful reform in Burma rests with the National League for Democracy (NLD) as led by Daw Aung San Suu Kyi, the ethnic nationalities, and the SPDC reaching a political settlement through dialogue. We remain deeply concerned that the United Nations–initiated talks between the NLD and the SPDC have not resumed and that U.N. Special Envoy Razali Ismail has not returned to Burma since meeting junta leader Than Shwe and Suu Kyi last November.

We reaffirm that the NLD is the sole legitimate representative of the people of Burma, having successfully competed against the military junta in parliamentary elections in May 1990. There are few more clear issues in Asia than the determined challenge to Burmese dictator Than Shwe by Suu Kyi.

The policy of the United States must be to continue to empower the NLD and Suu Kyi both in Burma and around the world. This requires regular and continuous consultation with the NLD and Suu Kyi on developments in Rangoon, the welfare of the people of Burma, and the provision of humanitarian assistance. It requires consultation and coordination with key allies in the struggle for freedom in Burma, including the British, ASEAN members, Japan, and other governments with economic ties to Burma, as well as others represented by the United Nations and codified and mandated in successive UN General Assembly resolutions. Further, it requires vigilance to ensure that no action by the U.S. government undermines the moral authority of the NLD.

Concurrent with this empowerment must be pressure on the SPDC to engage the NLD in dialogue and to end violations of human rights, including forced labor, rape, arrests, intimidation, and forced relocation of ethnic peoples from their indigenous lands. The dignity of the people of Burma needs to be addressed and restored. Sanctions, visa restrictions, support for democracy programs and activities, and regular reports by official and nongovernmental organizations on the repressive actions of the SPDC provide much needed leverage over the junta. Discussions on additional sanctions are underway.

Humanitarian assistance alone is not sufficient to safeguard the welfare of Burma's citizens. Absent the political will and interest of the SPDC to provide health care and education, such efforts are short-term fixes to longer-term problems. In considering such aid, international donors should examine the priorities of the SPDC as determined by their budgetary expenditures. It is unacceptable that the junta spends millions on arms deals at the expense of educational opportunities or access to health care for the Burmese and other ethnic minorities. Programs should be tailored to ensure that the beneficiaries of foreign aid dollars are not SPDC officials or their families.

The struggles of Nelson Mandela, Lech Walesa, Andrei Sakharov, and Vaclav Havel serve as evidence of the endurance—and triumph—of dedicated democrats. Some opine that it is not in the interests of the United States to support the aspirations of foreign nationals and integrate their hopes into official foreign policy. We do not share this view. It is our belief that, particularly in a country like Burma, where the people have chosen their leadership and democracy, it is incumbent on those of us serving as elected representatives to offer our unequivocal support to the elected representatives of the Burmese people. Freedom is not merely a philosophical concept, it is our foreign policy.

Dianne Feinstein, Tom Lantos,
Richard Lugar, Mitch McConnell

While I support increasing pressure on the regime in Burma, I also believe the United States should heed the lesson learned from earlier sanctions programs before embarking on new ones. The United States should work to develop multilateral sanctions first, before moving to a unilateral import ban. A unilateral ban would be minimally effective and will isolate U.S. policy. If a ban or other sanctions are imposed, the conditions that must be met to lift them should be precisely and publicly stated. Targeted sanctions can produce changed behavior if it is clear that the United States will not simply move goalposts when the regime does what we ask. In Burma it may be wise to stage different levels of sanctions relief to the release of political prisoners, and the restoration of credible talks on restoring democratic rule, and to stipulate positive incentives, such as a multilateral development program, that would result from new, free, and fair elections.

David L. Goldwyn

I wish to endorse the additional comments provided by David Steinberg, which are printed on pages 37–39.

James B. Heimowitz

I join all participants in desiring sustained progress toward democracy, transparency, and improved conditions within Myanmar (Burma). I concur with the report's recommendations urging more humanitarian aid for the Burmese people and for capacity training.

The report missed a valuable opportunity to fully explore options to support and provide impetus to ongoing diplomatic efforts or to evaluate U.S. policy alternatives. Task Force meetings (all occurring prior to the tragic May 30 events) barely addressed many key topics found in the report; others (e.g., border/refugee issues, U.S. policy vis-à-vis other governments, the UN) were never analyzed. Too easily dismissed or ignored were a range of initiatives that could help average Burmese *and* contribute to a process of lasting reform.

To prescribe additional U.S. trade sanctions without a serious discussion of their past impact or effectiveness is specious. Are additional sanctions the most efficacious use of diplomacy given limited positive results to date and the lack of concurrence by key trading nations? Have sanctions actually eroded U.S. influence? The harsh reality is that new trade sanctions will only worsen the plight of tens of thousands of workers and their families.

The pace of reform is frustrating; movement toward acceptance of international norms would be welcome. All should be concerned by recent events. Although some might find it tempting to replace diplomacy with isolation, this is precisely the time to have concerted engagement. We hope that circumstances will return quickly to a state where UN-brokered talks can resume *and* produce concrete results.

J. William Ichord

Socioeconomic and political conditions in Burma are deplorable; Burma's military governments since 1962 have misread their multiethnic society's needs, pursuing their national unity and development objectives with destructive results and with dire regional consequences.

But U.S. policy has been patently ineffective. This Task Force was a missed, rare opportunity to reexamine analytically policy options. U.S. concern about Burma is justified, but this report essentially reaffirms minimally effective U.S. policies. Listing many problems, it ignores U.S. multiple interests, neglecting evaluating U.S. strategic concerns—China, India, and ASEAN—and ignoring Burmese cooperation in terrorism and narcotics. Burma's role in and ASEAN's potential influence on Burma remain unaddressed. The report omits internal U.S. policy debates on Burma.

Sanctions have failed to mitigate political repression; economic mismanagement, corruption, and incompetence have injured the society more. Additional sanctions would be counterproductive, hurting hundreds of thousands without weakening military control. Reasserting the policy of recognizing the 1990 elections is a formula for failure (demanding regime change without incentives) and a romantic illusion.

Maintaining that the NLD is the legitimate government creates unaddressed diplomatic anomalies.

Denying Burma antinarcotics certification is a travesty given precipitous drops in opium production and lowered standards for certification to include Mexico. Isolation of Burma has been and remains an ineffective lever for change and is highly unlikely to succeed. Basic human-needs assistance through the UN and international NGOs is justified and urgently needed. Increased training and equitable treatment of Burmese in Thailand are essential. The country's two names—Burma and Myanmar—should be used pending political reconciliation.

The attack in central Burma on Aung San Suu Kyi and her entourage is deplorable. I am on record that there should be a public apology to the Burmese people by the military administration and the arrest of officers in charge and those perpetrators, since the Union Solidarity and Development Association is directly under military command. Both the United Nations and the ASEAN Regional Forum should consider the problem, but I continue to believe that sanctions and travel bans by the United States or the UN are not solutions. The military believe that they can withstand isolation. The natural endowments of that country once supported this conclusion in another era. This is no longer true. Technological communications, demographic growth, economic and political mismanagement have all changed that scenario. Isolation, internally or externally imposed, will no longer work and simply further pauperize the people without changing the regime. The United States should encourage the Japanese to stop the nonbasic human-needs aspects of their aid program and encourage Chinese reconsideration of their position. A thorough review of U.S. policy toward Burma in all its aspects is needed. This study is not a substitute for it.

David I. Steinberg

TASK FORCE MEMBERS

MAUREEN AUNG-THWIN is Director of the Burma Project/Southeast Asia Initiative of the Open Society Institute, which is part of the Soros Foundations Network. She currently serves on the advisory boards of Human Rights Watch/Asia and the Burma Studies Foundation, which oversees the Center for Burma Studies at Northern Illinois University.

JANET BENSHOOF is a human rights lawyer and the recipient of the MacArthur Fellows Award. She is also the President Emerita and founder of an international human rights organization, the Center for Reproductive Rights (formerly the Center for Reproductive Law and Policy). Currently she is teaching and working internationally on legal projects involving political equality, gender, security, and democracy issues.

GEORGE C. BIDDLE is Senior Vice President of the International Rescue Committee. Previously, he was Vice President of the International Crisis Group and President of the Institute for Central American Studies.

ROBERT CARSWELL is Of Counsel to Shearman & Sterling. From 1977 to 1981, he was Deputy Secretary of the Treasury under President Carter and also served as Chairman of the Carnegie Endowment for International Peace.

BOWMAN CUTTER is Managing Director at Warburg Pincus.

MATHEA FALCO, Chair of the Task Force, is President of Drug Strategies, a nonprofit research institute, and Associate Professor of Public Health at the Weill Medical College of Cornell University. She served as Assistant Secretary of State for International Narcotics Matters from 1977 to 1981.

Note: Task Force members participate in their individual and not institutional capacities.

*The individual has endorsed the report and submitted an additional or a dissenting view.

DIANNE FEINSTEIN* is the senior U.S. Senator from California. In 1992, she was elected with the most votes cast for a senator in U.S. history. She is the first woman to serve on the Senate Judiciary Committee and is the ranking member of the Technology and Terrorism Subcommittee and a member of the Select Committee on Intelligence.

ADRIENNE GERMAIN is President of the International Women's Health Coalition and has worked for 30 years on women's economic opportunities, health, and rights in southern countries. She is a member of the Asia and women's rights advisory committees of Human Rights Watch and of the Millennium Development Goals Project Task Force on Child Mortality and Maternal Health.

DAVID L. GOLDWYN* is President of Goldwyn International Strategies, LLC, an international consulting firm, and teaches the geopolitics of energy at Georgetown and Columbia Universities. He was Assistant Secretary of Energy for International Affairs and UN Ambassador Richardson's deputy on the National Security Council during the Clinton administration.

DONALD GREGG served in Burma with the U.S. embassy from 1964 to 1966. He was Ambassador to Republic of Korea from 1989 to 1993 and is now Chairman of the Korea Society.

JAMES B. HEIMOWITZ* is President and CEO of JBH Consulting Group, Inc., a New York–based consulting company that provides advice to Asia.

J. WILLIAM ICHORD* is Vice President of Government and International Relations for the Unocal Corporation. In this position he works on policy issues relevant to Southeast Asia and is an extensive traveler to the region.

EDWARD KLEIN is a contributing editor of *Vanity Fair* and a columnist for *Parade* magazine. Formerly, he was Editor in Chief of the *New York Times Magazine*. The author of two *New York Times* nonfiction best-sellers, he published a new book, *The Kennedy Curse*, in July 2003.

JOSHUA KURLANTZICK is Foreign Editor of the *New Republic*. Prior to working for the *New Republic*, Kurlantzick covered international politics and economics for *U.S. News and World Report* and has also covered Southeast Asia for *The Economist*.

TOM LANTOS* was elected to his twelfth term in the U.S House of Representatives in November 2002. He was first elected to Congress in November 1980. In 2001, he became the ranking Democratic member of the International Relations Committee. He is the only survivor of the Holocaust ever elected to Congress.

RICHARD LUGAR* is Chairman of the Senate Foreign Relations Committee and was elected to his fifth term in the Senate in 2000. He has been a leader in reducing the threat of nuclear, chemical, and biological weapons. To date, the Nunn-Lugar program has deactivated over 6,000 warheads that were once aimed at the United States.

TOM MALINOWSKI is the Washington Advocacy Director for Human Rights Watch. He was a Senior Director at the National Security Council from 1998 to 2001 and served at the State Department from 1994 to 1998.

MITCH MCCONNELL* is the U.S. Senate Majority Whip and Chairman of the Foreign Operations Subcommittee of the Senate Appropriations Committee.

ROBERT B. MILLMAN is the Saul P. Steinberg Distinguished Professor of Psychiatry and Public Health at the Weill Medical College of Cornell University. He is Director of Alcohol and Substance Abuse Services at the New York Presbyterian Hospital and currently is Chairman of the Board of Drug Strategies.

ARYEH NEIER is President of the Open Society Institute and the Soros Foundations Network. He previously served as Executive Director of Human Rights Watch.

---

*The individual has endorsed the report and submitted an additional or a dissenting view.

MARY ANNE SCHWALBE is the former Executive Director of the Women's Commission for Refugee Women and Children and serves on the board of the International Rescue Committee in the United Kingdom.

BROOKE L. SHEARER is a consultant. She was the first Executive Director of Yale University's World Fellows Program, directed the President's Commission on White House Fellowships, and initiated programs with the U.S. government and the World Bank to help emerging nations develop national parks and historical sites.

GEORGE SOROS is Chairman of Soros Fund Management LLC, a private investment management firm, and the founder of the Soros Foundations Network, a consortium of philanthropic organizations active in more than 50 countries. He is the author of seven books, most recently *George Soros on Globalization*.

DAVID I. STEINBERG* is Distinguished Professor and Director of Asian Studies at the Walsh School of Foreign Service at Georgetown University. He is the author of four books and 45 articles on Burma/Myanmar, the latest book being *Burma: The State of Myanmar*. He has also written extensively on Korean affairs.

ROSE STYRON is a poet, journalist, and human rights activist who has chaired Amnesty International's National Advisory Council, PEN's Freedom-to-Write Committee, and the Robert F. Kennedy Human Rights Awards.

MONA SUTPHEN is Managing Director of Stonebridge International LLC. As a Foreign Service Officer, she served at the National Security Council as Special Assistant to National Security Adviser Samuel Berger and as an adviser to U.S. Ambassador to the UN Bill Richardson. She also worked extensively on Burmese policy issues during stints with the U.S. embassy in Bangkok.

KENNETH WOLLACK is President of the National Democratic Institute for International Affairs.

TASK FORCE OBSERVERS

MORTON I. ABRAMOWITZ
The Century Foundation

JOHN BRANDON
The Asia Foundation

MATTHEW P. DALEY
U.S. Department of State

NANCY ELY-RAPHEL
U.S. Department of State

ERIC P. SCHWARTZ
Council on Foreign Relations

CHRISTOPHER H. SMITH
U.S. House of Representatives

NANCY E. SODERBERG
International Crisis Group

DANILO TURK
United Nations Department of Political Affairs

APPENDIXES

APPENDIX A: UNITED NATIONS GENERAL ASSEMBLY RESOLUTION

United Nations   A/C.3/57/L.48

General Assembly   Distr.: Limited
                                    2 November 2002

Original: English

Fifty-seventh session
Third Committee
Agenda item 109 (c)
Human rights questions: human rights situations and
reports of special rapporteurs and representatives

Albania, Andorra, Australia, Austria, Belgium, Bulgaria, Canada, Costa Rica, Czech Republic, Denmark, Estonia, Finland,
France, Germany, Greece, Hungary, Iceland, Ireland, Italy,
Latvia, Liechtenstein, Lithuania, Luxembourg, Malta, Mona-
co, Netherlands, New Zealand, Norway, Poland, Portugal,
Republic of Korea, Romania, San Marino, Slovenia, Spain, Swe-
den, Switzerland, United Kingdom of Great Britain and Northern Ireland and United States of America:
draft resolution

Situation of human rights in Myanmar

The General Assembly,

Guided by the Charter of the United Nations, the Universal
Declaration of Human Rights,[1] the International Covenants on
Human Rights[2] and other human rights instruments,

Reaffirming that all States Members of the United Nations have
an obligation to promote and protect human rights and fundamental

---

[1]Resolution 217 A (III).
[2]Resolution 2200 A (XXI), annex.

freedoms and to fulfil the obligations they have undertaken under the various international instruments in the field,

Aware that Myanmar is a party to the Convention on the Rights of the Child,[3] the Convention on the Elimination of All Forms of Discrimination against Women,[4] the Geneva Conventions of 12 August 1949 on the protection of the victims of war,[5] as well as the Convention concerning forced or compulsory labour (Convention No. 29) of 1930 and the Convention concerning freedom of association and protection of the right to organize (Convention No. 87) of 1948 of the International Labour Organization,

Recalling its previous resolutions on the subject, the most recent of which is resolution 56/231 of 24 December 2001, and those of the Commission on Human Rights, the most recent of which is resolution 2002/67 of 25 April 2002,[6]

Recalling resolution I adopted by the International Labour Conference at its eighty-eighth session, on 14 June 2000, concerning the practice of forced or compulsory labour in Myanmar,

Affirming that the will of the people is the basis of the authority of government and that the will of the people of Myanmar was clearly expressed in the elections held in 1990,

Affirming also that the establishment of a genuine democratic government in Myanmar is essential for the realization of all human rights and fundamental freedoms,

1. *Welcomes*:

(a) The preliminary steps taken by the Government of Myanmar towards democracy, in particular: the release from house arrest of Aung San Suu Kyi on 6 May 2002 and her subsequent internal freedom of movement, the release of a number of polit-

---

[3]Resolution 44/25, annex.
[4]Resolution 34/180, annex.
[5]United Nations, *Treaty Series*, vol. 75, Nos. 970–973.
[6]See *Official Records of the Economic and Social Council, 2002, Supplement No. 3* (E/2002/23), chap. II, sect. A

ical prisoners, and the relaxation of some constraints on some political activities of the National League for Democracy;

(b) The appointment by the International Labour Organization of a liaison officer in Myanmar as a first step towards the establishment of full and effective representation of the Organization in Myanmar;

(c) The visits to Myanmar by the Special Envoy of the Secretary-General on Myanmar during the past year, and the visits by the Special Rapporteur of the Commission on Human Rights on the situation of human rights in Myanmar, and the cooperation extended to them by the Government of Myanmar;

(d) The continued cooperation with the International Committee of the Red Cross;

(e) The dissemination of human rights standards for public officials and some non-governmental organizations and ethnic groups through a series of human rights workshops;

2. *Notes* the establishment by the Government of Myanmar of a committee on human rights as a precursor to the establishment of a national human rights commission, which would follow the Principles relating to the status of national institutions for the promotion and protection of human rights annexed to General Assembly resolution 48/134 of 20 December 1993;

3. *Expresses its grave concern* at:

(a) The ongoing systematic violation of the human rights, including civil, political, economic, social and cultural rights, of the people of Myanmar;

(b) Extrajudicial killings; rapes and other forms of sexual violence carried out by members of the armed forces; torture; renewed instances of political arrests and continuing detentions, including of prisoners whose sentences have expired; forced relocation; destruction of livelihoods; forced labour; denial of freedoms of assembly, association, expression and movement; discrimination on the basis of religious or ethnic background; wide disrespect for the rule of law and lack of independence of the judiciary; deeply unsatisfactory conditions of detention; systematic use of child soldiers; and violations of the rights to an adequate standard of living, in particular food and medical care, and to education;

(c) The disproportionate suffering of members of ethnic minorities, women and children from such violations;

(d) The situation of the large number of internally displaced persons and the flow of refugees to neighbouring countries;

(e) The ever-increasing impact of the human immunodeficiency virus/acquired immunodeficiency syndrome (HIV/AIDS) on the population of Myanmar;

4. *Calls upon* the Government of Myanmar:

(a) To fulfill its obligations to restore the independence of the judiciary and due process of law, and to take further steps to reform the system of the administration of justice;

(b) To take immediate action to implement fully concrete legislative, executive and administrative measures to eradicate the practice of forced labour and to implement fully the recommendations of the Commission of Inquiry established to examine the observance by Myanmar of the International Labour Organization Convention concerning forced or compulsory labour (Convention No. 29) of 1930;

(c) To pursue the dialogue with the International Labour Organization towards the implementation of a full and effective representation of the organization in Myanmar;

(d) To ensure safe and unhindered access to the United Nations and international humanitarian organizations and to cooperate fully with all sectors of society, especially with the National League for Democracy and other relevant political, ethnic and community-based groups through consultation, to ensure the provision of humanitarian assistance and to guarantee that it actually reaches the most vulnerable groups of the population;

(e) To continue to cooperate with the Special Envoy of the Secretary-General on Myanmar and the Special Rapporteur of the Commission on Human Rights on the situation of human rights in Myanmar;

(f) To consider as a matter of high priority becoming a party to: the International Covenant on Civil and Political Rights,[7] the International Covenant on Economic, Social and Cultural Rights,[8] the Convention against Torture and Other Cruel, Inhuman or Degrading Treatment or Punishment,[9] the International Convention on the Elimination of All Forms of Racial Discrimination,[10] the Convention relating to the Status of Refugees[11] and its Protocol,[12] the Optional Protocol on the involvement of children in armed conflict[13] to the Convention on the Rights of the Child[14] and the International Labour Organization Convention concerning the prohibition and immediate action for the elimination of the worst forms of child labour (Convention No. 182) of 1999;

(g) To pursue through dialogue and peaceful means an end to conflict with all ethnic groups in Myanmar;

5. *Strongly urges* the Government of Myanmar:

(a) To restore democracy and implement the results of the 1990 elections and to ensure that the contacts with Aung San Suu Kyi and other leaders of the National League for Democracy move without delay into substantive and structured dialogue towards democratization and national reconciliation and at an early stage to include other political leaders in these talks, including the representatives of the ethnic groups;

---

[7]See note 2.
[8]See note 2.
[9]Resolution 39/46, annex.
[10]Resolution 34/180, annex.
[11]United Nations, *Treaty Series,* vol. 189, No. 2545.
[12]Ibid., vol. 606, No. 8791.
[13]Resolution 54/263, annex I.
[14]See note 3.

(b) To end the systematic violations of human rights in Myanmar and to ensure full respect for all human rights and fundamental freedoms and, to end impunity, to investigate and bring to justice any perpetrators of human rights violations, including members of the military and other government agents in all circumstances;

(c) To facilitate and cooperate fully with an independent international investigation of charges of rapes and other abuse of civilians carried out by members of the armed forces in Shan and other states;

(d) To release unconditionally and immediately all political prisoners;

(e) To put an immediate end to the recruitment and use of child soldiers and to extend full cooperation to relevant international organizations in order to ensure the demobilization of child soldiers, their return home and their rehabilitation;

(f) To lift all restraints on peaceful political activity, including guaranteeing freedom of association and freedom of expression, including freedom of the media;

(g) To end the systematic enforced displacement of persons and other causes of refugee flows to neighbouring countries, and to provide the necessary protection and assistance to internally displaced persons and to respect the right of refugees to voluntary, safe and dignified return monitored by appropriate international agencies;

(h) To recognize further the gravity of the situation regarding HIV/AIDS and the need to take necessary action against the epidemic, including through the effective implementation in Myanmar of the United Nations joint action plan on HIV/AIDS, in cooperation with all relevant political and ethnic groups;

6. *Requests* the Secretary-General to continue to provide his good offices and to pursue his discussions on the situation of human rights and the restoration of democracy with the Government and people of Myanmar, to submit additional reports to the General Assembly during its fifty-seventh session on the progress of those

discussions, and to report to the Assembly at its fifty-eighth session and to the Commission on Human Rights at its fifty-ninth session on the progress made in the implementation of the present resolution;

7. *Decides* to continue consideration of this question at its fifty-eighth session.

APPENDIX B: EUROPEAN UNION COMMON POSITION

(Acts adopted pursuant to Title V of the Treaty on European Union)

COUNCIL COMMON POSITION 2003/297/CFSP
of 28 April 2003
on Burma/Myanmar

THE COUNCIL OF THE EUROPEAN UNION,

Having regard to the Treaty on European Union, and in particular Article 15 thereof,

Whereas:

(1) On 28 October 1996, the Council adopted Common Position 96/635/CFSP on Burma/Myanmar,[1] which expires on 29 April 2003.

(2) In view of the further deterioration in the political situation in Burma/Myanmar, as witnessed by the failure of the military authorities to enter into substantive discussions with the democratic movement concerning a process leading to national reconciliation, respect for human rights and democracy and the continuing serious violations of human rights, including the failure to take action to eradicate the use of forced labour in accordance with the recommendations of the International Labour Organisation's High-Level Team report of 2001, the Council has deemed it necessary to further expand and strengthen the measures taken under Common Position 96/635/CFSP against the military regime in Burma/Myanmar, those who benefit most from its misrule and those who actively frustrate the process of national reconciliation, respect for human rights and democracy.

---

[1]OJ L 287, 8.11.1996, p.1. Common Position at last amended by Common Position 2002/831/CFSP (OJ L 285, 23.10.2002, p. 7).

(3) Accordingly the scope of the visa ban and assets freeze should be extended to include further members of the military regime, the military and security forces, the military regime's economic interests and other individuals, groups, undertakings or entities associated with the military regime who formulate, implement or benefit from policies that impede Burma/Myanmar's transition to democracy and their families and associates.

(4) The Council also deems it necessary to modify the arms embargo to prohibit technical training or assistance.

(5) The Council has decided to suspend the extension of the visa ban and assets freeze, along with the prohibition of technical training or assistance under the arms embargo, up to 29 October 2003 at the latest. Those measures will not be imposed if by that time there is substantive progress towards national reconciliation, the restoration of a democratic order and greater respect for human rights in Burma/Myanmar.

(6) Exemptions should be introduced in the arms embargo in order to allow the export of certain military rated equipment for humanitarian use.

(7) The implementation of the visa ban should be without prejudice to cases where a Member State is bound by an obligation of international law, or is host country of the Organisation for Security and Cooperation in Europe (OSCE), or where the Minister and Vice-Minister for Foreign Affairs for Burma/Myanmar visit with prior notification and agreement of the Council.

(8) The implementation of the ban on high level visits at the level of Political Director and above should be without prejudice to the Troika visit scheduled to take place before 29 October 2003 provided certain conditions are met, and to cases where the European Union decides that the visit is directly in pursuit of national reconciliation, respect for human rights and democracy in Burma/Myanmar.

(9) Action by the Community is needed in order to implement certain measures.

(10) In the light of the above developments, Common Position 96/635/CFSP should be repealed and replaced,

HAS ADOPTED THIS COMMON POSITION:

Article 1

All military personnel attached to the diplomatic representations of Burma/Myanmar in Member States shall be expelled and all military personnel attached to diplomatic representations of the Member States in Burma/Myanmar shall be withdrawn.

Article 2

1. An embargo on arms, munitions and military equipment shall be enforced against Myanmar[2].

2. The provision to Burma/Myanmar of technical training or assistance related to the provision, manufacture, maintenance or use of the items mentioned in paragraph 1 by nationals of Member States or from the territories of the Member States, shall be prohibited.

3. Paragraphs 1 and 2 shall not apply to supplies of nonlethal military equipment intended solely for humanitarian or protective use, and related technical assistance or training, nor shall they apply to protective clothing, including flak jackets and military helmets, temporarily exported to Burma/Myanmar by United Nations personnel, representatives of the media and humanitarian and development workers and associated personnel for their personal use only.

Article 3

Non-humanitarian aid or development programmes shall be suspended. Exceptions may be made for projects and programmes which should be, as far as possible, defined in consultation with democratic groups, including the National League for Democracy, and run with their involvement:

---

[2] The aforementioned embargo covers weapons designed to kill and their ammunition, weapon platforms, non-weapon platforms and ancillary equipment. The embargo also covers spare parts, repairs, maintenance and transfer of military technology. Contracts entered into prior to 8 November 1996 are not affected by this Common Position.

— in support of human rights and democracy,
— in support of poverty alleviation and, in particular, of the provision of basic needs for the poorest section of the population, in the context of decentralised cooperation through local civilian authorities and non-governmental organisations,
— in support of health and basic education through non-governmental organisations.

Article 4

1. Member States shall take the necessary measures to prevent the entry into, or transit through, the territories of senior members of the State Peace and Development Council (SPDC), Burmese authorities in the tourism sector, senior members of the military, the Government or the security forces who formulate, implement or benefit from policies that impede Burma/Myanmars transition to democracy, and their families.

2. The persons to which paragraph 1 applies are those listed in the Annex.

3. Paragraph 1 will not oblige a Member State to refuse its own nationals entry to its territory.

4. Paragraph 1 shall be without prejudice to the cases where a Member State is bound by an obligation of international law, namely:
(a) as a host country of an international intergovernmental organisation;
(b) as a host country to an international conference convened by, or under the auspices of, the Untied Nations; or
(c) under a multilateral agreement conferring privileges and immunities.

The Council shall be duly informed in each of these cases.

5. Paragraph 4 shall be considered as applying also in cases where a Member State is host of the OSCE.

6. Member States may grant exemptions from the measures imposed in paragraph 1 where travel is justified on the grounds of

urgent humanitarian need, or on grounds of attending inter-governmental meetings, including those promoted by the European Union, where a political dialogue is conducted that directly promotes democracy, human rights and the rule of law in Burma/Myanmar.

7. A Member State wishing to grant exemptions from measures imposed under paragraph 6 shall notify the Council in writing. The exemption will be deemed to be granted unless one or more of the Council Members raises an objection in writing within 48 hours of receiving notification of the proposed exemption. In the event that one or more of the Council members raises an objection, the Council, acting by qualified majority, may decide to grant the proposed exemption.

8. In cases where, pursuant to paragraphs 4, 5, 6 and 7, a Member State authorises the entry into, or transit through, its territory of persons listed in the Annex, the authorisation shall be limited to the purpose for which it is given and to the persons concerned thereby.

Article 5

Funds held abroad by persons referred to in Article 4(1), as identified in the Annex, will be frozen.

Article 6

No equipment which might be used for internal repression or terrorism will be supplied to Burma/Myanmar.

Article 7

Without prejudice to the Troika visit, scheduled to take place provided certain conditions are met, high-level bilateral governmental (Ministers and Officials at the level of Political Director and above) visits to Burma/Myanmar shall be suspended. The Council may, in exceptional circumstances, decide to grant exceptions to this rule.

Article 8

The Council, acting upon a proposal by a Member State or the Commission, shall adopt modifications to the list contained in the Annex as required.

Article 9

Unless the Council decides otherwise:

(a) sanctions set out in this Common Position shall, no later than 29 October 2003, be extended to include further members of the military regime, the military and security forces, the military regime's economic interests and other individuals, groups, undertakings or entities associated with the military regime who formulate, implement or benefit from policies that impede Burma/Myanmar's transition to democracy, and their families and associates.

(b) the provisions of Article 2(2) shall remain suspended until 29 October 2003.

Article 10

1. The implementation of this Common Position will be monitored by the Council and will be reviewed in the light of developments in Burma/Myanmar. Further measures may need to be considered.

2. In the case of a substantial improvement of the overall political situation in Burma/Myanmar, not only the suspension of the aforementioned measures, but also the gradual resumption of cooperation with Burma/Myanmar will be considered, after assessment of developments by the Council.

Article 11

Common Position 96/635/CFSP is hereby repealed and shall be replaced by this Common Position. Existing references to Common Position 96/635/CFSP shall be read as references to this Common Position.

Article 12

This Common Position shall take effect on the date of its adoption. It shall expire on 29 April 2004.

Article 13

This Common Position shall be published in the *Official Journal of the European Union.*

Done at Brussels, 28 April 2003.

For the Council

The President

G. PAPANDREOU

SELECTED REPORTS OF INDEPENDENT TASK FORCES
SPONSORED BY THE COUNCIL ON FOREIGN RELATIONS

* †*Emergency Responders: Drastically Underfunded, Dangerously Unprepared* (2003)
Warren B. Rudman, Chair; Richard A. Clarke, Senior Adviser; Jamie F. Metzl,
Project Director

* †*Meeting the North Korean Nuclear Challenge* (2003)
Morton I. Abramowitz and James T. Laney, Co-Chairs; Eric Heginbotham,
Project Director

* †*Chinese Military Power* (2003)
Harold Brown, Chair; Joseph W. Prueher, Vice Chair; Adam Segal,
Project Director

* †*Iraq: The Day After* (2003)
Thomas R. Pickering and James R. Schlesinger, Co-Chairs; Eric P.
Schwartz, Project Director

* †*Threats to Democracy* (2002)
Madeleine K. Albright and Bronislaw Geremek, Co-Chairs; Morton H.
Halperin, Project Director; Elizabeth Frawley Bagley, Associate Director

* †*America—Still Unprepared, Still in Danger* (2002)
Gary Hart and Warren B. Rudman, Co-Chairs; Stephen Flynn, Project Director

* †*Terrorist Financing* (2002)
Maurice R. Greenberg, Chair; William F. Wechsler and Lee S. Wolosky, Project
Co-Directors

* †*Enhancing U.S. Leadership at the United Nations* (2002)
David Dreier and Lee H. Hamilton, Co-Chairs; Lee Feinstein and Adrian Karat-
nycky, Project Co-Directors

* †*Testing North Korea: The Next Stage in U.S. and ROK Policy (2001)*
Morton I. Abramowitz and James T. Laney, Co-Chairs; Robert A. Manning,
Project Director

* †*The United States and Southeast Asia: A Policy Agenda for the New Administration*
(2001)
J. Robert Kerrey, Chair; Robert A. Manning, Project Director

* †*Strategic Energy Policy: Challenges for the 21st Century* (2001)
Edward L. Morse, Chair; Amy Myers Jaffe, Project Director

* †*State Department Reform* (2001)
Frank C. Carlucci, Chair; Ian J. Brzezinski, Project Coordinator;
Cosponsored with the Center for Strategic and International Studies

* †*U.S.-Cuban Relations in the 21st Century: A Follow-on Report* (2001)
Bernard W. Aronson and William D. Rogers, Co-Chairs; Julia Sweig and Walter
Mead, Project Directors

* †*A Letter to the President and a Memorandum on U.S. Policy Toward Brazil* (2001)
Stephen Robert, Chair; Kenneth Maxwell, Project Director

* †*Toward Greater Peace and Security in Colombia* (2000)
Bob Graham and Brent Scowcroft, Co-Chairs; Michael Shifter, Project Director;
Cosponsored with the Inter-American Dialogue

†*Future Directions for U.S. Economic Policy Toward Japan* (2000)
Laura D'Andrea Tyson, Chair; M. Diana Helweg Newton, Project Director

* †*Promoting Sustainable Economies in the Balkans* (2000)
Steven Rattner, Chair; Michael B. G. Froman, Project Director

* †*Nonlethal Technologies: Progress and Prospects* (1999)
Richard L. Garwin, Chair; W. Montague Winfield, Project Director

* †*U.S. Policy Toward North Korea: Next Steps* (1999)
Morton I. Abramowitz and James T. Laney, Co-Chairs; Michael J. Green, Project
Director

†*Safeguarding Prosperity in a Global Financial System: The Future International Finan-
cial Architecture* (1999)
Carla A. Hills and Peter G. Peterson, Co-Chairs; Morris Goldstein, Project
Director

---

†Available on the Council on Foreign Relations website at www.cfr.org.
*Available from Brookings Institution Press. To order, call 800-275-1447.